CITIES OF THE
WORLD

ROME

BY R. CONRAD STEIN

CHILDREN'S PRESS®
A Division of Grolier Publishing
New York London Hong Kong Sydney
Danbury, Connecticut

CONSULTANTS

Edward Muir, Ph.D.
Clarence Ver Steeg Professor in the Arts and Sciences
Department of History
Northwestern University

Linda Cornwell
Learning Resource Consultant
Indiana Department of Education

Project Editor: Downing Publishing Services
Design Director: Karen Kohn & Associates, Ltd.
Photo Researcher: Jan Izzo
Pronunciations: Courtesy of Tony Breed, M.A., Linguistics, University of Chicago

NOTES ON ITALIAN PRONUNCIATION
Most of the pronunciations in this book are exactly as they look, with the
following notes: *ah* and *o* are like *a* in father; *a* is as in can; *ar* is as in far; *ai* and
ay are like *ai* in rain; *aw* is as in draw; *u* and *uh* are like *u* in but; *igh* is as in
light; *oh* and *oa* are like *oa* in boat; *oo* is as in food. In Italian, if two
consonants are written in a row, the consonant should be pronounced longer—
a little like the *ts* in the English phrase "eat two." The Italian words *coca* and
cocca should sound different; *coca* is "koh-kah" and *cocca* is "koak-kah."

Library of Congress Cataloging-in-Publication Data
Stein, R. Conrad.
      Rome / by R. Conrad Stein.
        p.   cm. — (Cities of the world)
      Includes bibliographical references and index.
      Summary: Discusses the history, culture, daily life, food, people, sports,
and points of interest of the city that was once the capital of the mighty
Roman Empire.
    ISBN 0-516-20465-3 (lib. bdg.)   0-516-26240-8 (pbk.)
    1. Rome (Italy) — Juvenile literature. [l. Rome (Italy)]
I. Title. II. Series: Cities of the world (New York, N.Y.)
DG804.2.S74   1997
937'. 6—dc21

96-54633
CIP
AC

TABLE OF CONTENTS

"All roads lead to Rome." Every European language has its own version of this old saying. For ages, it seemed to Europeans that Rome was the center of the universe. The city was once the capital of the most powerful empire ever known. Catholics have always viewed Rome as the centerpiece of their religion. Rome is a living museum where the works of Europe's greatest artists and architects stand. It is also a city of music, friendliness, and great food. Tourists from all over the world come to Rome each year. The expression "All roads lead to Rome" is as appropriate now as it was when first said hundreds of years ago.

One historic road leading to the city is called the Via Appia, the Appian Way. Soldiers in glittering armor once paraded over the Appian Way to enter Rome in triumph. Saint Peter walked this road only to be executed in Rome. The Appian Way still leads to the heart of the city. Cars, trucks, and motorcycles now roar over the roadway. Amazingly, many of the paving stones embedded in the Appian Way were placed there by Roman workers some 2,000 years ago. This is Rome. It is a place as modern as today, yet as old as a legend.

Another old expression says, "Rome wasn't built in a day." Quite true. It can't be seen in a day or studied in a day either. Yet even a brief look at Rome is a thrilling experience. The many charms of the Italian capital fascinate students as well as vacationers.

Above: The Sant' Angelo Bridge over the Tiber River
Left: A section of the Via Appia
Opposite page: The Colosseum, with the colonnade in the foreground

Via Appia
(VEE-AH OPP-EE-AH)

There are hundreds of theaters in Rome. They include movie theaters, legitimate theaters, operas, and puppet performances put on in parks. But the city's liveliest theater takes place every day on the streets. Rome's gentle climate encourages outdoor living. The city hosts an exciting world of street vendors, street musicians, and open-air markets. Simply by going about their everyday activities, the people of Rome create a theater in the streets. It is free entertainment. And the streets welcome all.

A DAY IN THE ROMAN THEATER

Rome's streets come to life in late morning, when people begin the task of shopping. The city has few supermarkets that sell a variety of goods all under one roof. Instead, shoppers go to one tiny store for meat, another for vegetables, and still another to buy bread. Many food vendors operate stalls in a neighborhood marketplace. When a shopper enters a store or approaches a stall, the owner says a warm *"Buon giorno!"* ("Good morning!"). Then the theater begins. In the vegetable store, the shopkeeper holds up a head of lettuce and says, "Buy here. I have the freshest vegetables in town."

Many shoppers stop for a snack. *Pizza bianca* (white pizza) is a morning treat. It consists of a pizza crust covered with olive oil and just a dash of tomato. In marketplaces, people often eat standing up in front of a tiny restaurant counter. They chat with neighbors or with the restaurant owner. In some ways, marketplaces are large meeting halls. Customers come to socialize as well as to shop.

Roman food vendors operate stalls in neighborhood marketplaces like this one.

A butcher shop on the Via del Corso

In the city's old sections, people pass ancient statues that are embedded in the walls of buildings. The statues are like stone pages of a history book. They remind passersby that Rome was once the center of the mightiest empire on earth. Remains of the golden past are encased in the buildings used by modern Romans every day. Columns from an ancient temple stand near a stall in an open-air market. The walls of a simple barbershop are graced with slabs of marble that came from a centuries-old palace. Art historians and tourists study these objects of the past that are part of the modern city. Romans themselves rarely pause to look at the ancient columns and statues. They are decorations in the wonderful theater of their city.

Pizza bianca with pepper, onion, and olives

Night provides the last act of the Roman theater. Romans believe in staying up late. Not too many years ago, the typical Roman took a *siesta* after lunch. Armed with this nap, the Roman enjoyed the city's many fine restaurants until well after midnight. Today, the siesta tradition has faded. Still, the streets are alive with people until late in the evening. At twilight, the street entertainers—including jugglers and puppeteers—make their appearance. Small children are entranced by the puppets. The hand-held puppets wrestle and punch each other, but in the end always kiss and make up. Older children play pickup soccer games in the narrow, twisting alleys. A streetlight illuminates their makeshift soccer field. Two parked cars serve as goal posts. At about midnight, the curtain begins to close on Rome's theater of the streets. But the show will start again the next morning, and the next, and the next.

This little girl is delighted by a puppet show in a Rome Park.

Clown puppet

A street entertainer in Piazza Barberini

siesta (SEE-ESS-tAH)
pasta (PAH-STAH)

Cats

Some senior residents of Rome are the hordes of cats that live in the old sections. In the year 30 B.C., Rome conquered the cat-loving nation of Egypt. Roman soldiers brought back a few felines as pets. They have thrived in the city ever since. Most are strays, belonging to no one. Yet the cats are fed regularly. Old women often bring them plates of leftover *pasta* and scraps of meat.

THE HAZARDS

Yes, there are villains in the great Roman theater. Petty thieves and pickpockets work their mischief on the streets. Sadly, some of the criminals are children. The underage thieves often pick on tourists. One of their favorite tricks is to have a particularly ragged-looking child rub his belly and point to his open mouth. The routine indicates the boy is starving. When the tourist's back is turned, two others will snatch a handbag or run away with a suitcase. The young outlaws are athletic and hard to catch. Sometimes they are called *scugnizzi*, from an Italian word meaning "to spin like a top."

Traffic is a far more menacing villain than the occasional thief. Cars roar at pedestrians from every direction. People on foot leave the sidewalks only at their own peril. Even this tactic, however, does not ensure one's safety. Roman drivers frequently park on the sidewalks. When caught in traffic, some motorists even drive along the walkways.

More than a million cars, trucks, and buses swarm into Rome every day. The streets snake this way and that to wind around Rome's ancient landmark buildings. This situation results in constant traffic jams and a frightening number of car crashes. Usually, the accidents produce only minor damage because cars move at the pace of a crawling worm. But a fender-bender can become an episode in street theater. After a crash, drivers jump out to inspect the damage to their cars. Arms wave wildly. Accusations and curses fly. Each driver blames the other. Then a member of the Roman police force appears—sharply dressed in a tan or blue uniform. The policeman is a picture of calm as he talks to the raging drivers. After all, the police officer is another actor in the city's theater. He must play his role.

A Roman policeman directing heavy traffic

scugnizzi (SKOO-NYEET-SEE)

Heavy automobile traffic at the Piazza Venezia

Mopeds

Traffic jams are so bad that many Romans own a moped in addition to a car. The motorbikes allow people to weave through the paralyzed traffic on the streets. Even wealthy bankers in business suits and women wearing expensive fur coats are seen scooting about the city on mopeds.

Julius Caesar (JOO-lee-uss SEE-zer)
Colosseum (CAH-LUH-SEE-umm)

Some 2,000 years ago, Roman emperor Julius Caesar banned all traffic from the center of Rome. Caesar believed the animal-drawn wagons clogging the streets brought too much confusion to his city. Authorities in modern Rome are following Caesar's ancient example. Each year, more and more areas of the city are proclaimed off-limits to cars. Many motorists grumble about the restrictions. Romans have a love affair with their automobiles. With great pride, they shine fenders and polish bumper chrome. Some car owners believe the city should be altered to create new highways. A story is told about an American tourist riding in a taxicab. The tourist pointed out the window and said, "Wow, there's the Colosseum." The Colosseum is a famous stadium built during the glory days of ancient Rome. The cab driver—who was stuck in a stubborn traffic jam—said, "Yes, the Colosseum, and it ought to be torn down. It blocks traffic."

ISLANDS IN THE CITY

Rome is blessed with scores of *piazzas* (town squares). They are open areas where people can relax on benches. Piazzas are islands, safe from traffic. For families, the piazzas serve as both a living room and a backyard. When several families get together, they often meet in a piazza instead of in a home. On piazza grounds, small children run between the benches playing tag. Teenagers walk together and flirt. Outdoor restaurants ring the streets surrounding the piazzas. Paris is famous for its outdoor cafes, but Rome probably has more of them.

One of the most popular squares is the Piazza di Spagna. It is nearly always crowded with Romans and tourists. The Spanish Steps, a famous Rome landmark, is the most striking feature of the piazza. The Spanish Steps is a graceful cascade of stairs leading from an ornate church down to the piazza. In the Piazza di Spagna, native Romans hardly notice the swarms of tourists. For hundreds of years, foreigners have come to this piazza and to other famous locations in the Italian capital. Tourists are part of Rome's everyday life. The foreigners are spectators in the city's great theater.

Long ago, the piazzas were designed to impress visitors. Most were financed by popes, leaders of the Roman Catholic Church. The popes hoped to delight people making religious pilgrimages to Rome. Church authorities commissioned Italy's greatest architects to lay out grand squares where major streets intersected.

The Spanish Steps at the Piazza di Spagna is a favorite resting place for Romans and tourists.

The Piazza San Pietro (St. Peter's Square) was completed in 1656 as a spectacular entranceway to St. Peter's Basilica (church). The Piazza del Popolo was built to greet visitors approaching from the north. Today, the Piazza del Popolo is a favorite place for young people to get together.

The Piazza Navona is beloved by Romans. Handsome old houses, some with roof gardens, look over the square. The square has an unspoiled feeling. It hasn't changed much since the seventeenth century. Piazza Navona is even older than it seems. It is a rectangular piazza, with curved ends. This shape comes from the fact that it was once a course where ancient Romans held chariot races. The Piazza Navona is a striking example of today's Rome shaped by its long-ago past.

Fountain of the Four Rivers, in the Piazza Navona

This child with a bicycle in the Piazza di Spagna must have felt very small next to these large, handsome horses.

piazza (PYOTT-sah)
Piazza di Spagna
(PYOTT-sah dee SPAH-nyah)
Piazza San Pietro (PYOTT-sah sahn PYAY-troh)
Basilica (BAH-ZEE-lee-kah)
Piazza del Popolo (PYOTT-sah dail POH-poh-loh)
Piazza Navona
(PYOTT-sah nah-VOH-nah)

ome is so old that its origins are lost in legend. The most popular legend says the city was laid out in 753 B.C. by twin brothers, Romulus and Remus. The legend further claims that the god Mars was the father of the twins, and that they were once nursed by a female wolf. Rome is often called the Eternal City because it has been so important through the ages.

Romulus (ROMM-yoo-luss)
Remus (REE-muss)

OLD ROME

The old city of Rome was shaped by the Tiber River and by seven small hills. The Tiber is still a major feature of Rome. The seven hills are now covered with structures and can barely be distinguished by modern Romans. Some 2,000 years ago, the great Roman Empire stretched from present-day England to the Sahara Desert in Africa. At its height, Rome's territory embraced about one-fourth of Europe and much of the Middle East.

The capital city of this vast empire was magnificent to behold. White marble statues stood in its piazzas. Buildings were supported by graceful columns. Public baths were popular gathering spots for the city dwellers. The baths looked like large swimming pools. Political life centered on a marketplace called the Forum. At the Forum, Roman leaders assembled to attend meetings.

This eighteenth-century engraving by Giambattista Piranesi makes Isola Tiberina (the island in the Tiber River) look like a ship.

Tiber (TIGH-ber)

Forum (FOAR-umm)

Above: A detail of the carvings on Trajan's column
Right: A statue of Roman emperor Trajan

Rich and powerful Romans tried to outdo one another by creating monuments to their own glory. One such Roman was the Emperor Trajan, who ruled beginning in A.D. 98. Trajan's Column can be seen today. The towering column is covered with carvings that celebrate Trajan's military victories.

Trajan (TRAY-jen)

The greatest of all ancient Roman ruins is the Colosseum, completed in A.D. 80. The massive stadium could seat as many as 70,000 people. On the sands of the arena, gladiators fought to the death. If a gladiator shrank from combat, he was prodded forward with whips or red-hot irons. Public executions were grim spectacles at the Colosseum. Lawbreakers—both men and women—were thrown into the arena with lions that had been deliberately starved. On some occasions, the Colosseum grounds were flooded and slaves staged sea battles complete with vicious sword fighting. During the mock combat, the waters turned red with blood. Romans stood in the stands, wildly cheering these gory displays. One Roman wrote, "Such a throng flocked to these shows that . . . the press was such that many were crushed to death."

The Roman Empire declined in the A.D. 400s. Without Rome's leadership, Europe entered a historical period called the Middle Ages. During the Middle Ages, roughly from the 400s to the 1400s, European civilization lost much of the knowledge once held by Rome. The city of Rome was torn by war and poverty. Its population fell from about 1 million during its glory years to 13,000 by the fourteenth century. The great buildings of old Rome became ruins, ghosts of the past.

Yet the seeds of a new Rome were planted even before the old empire collapsed. After the death of Jesus Christ, Saint Peter traveled to Rome.

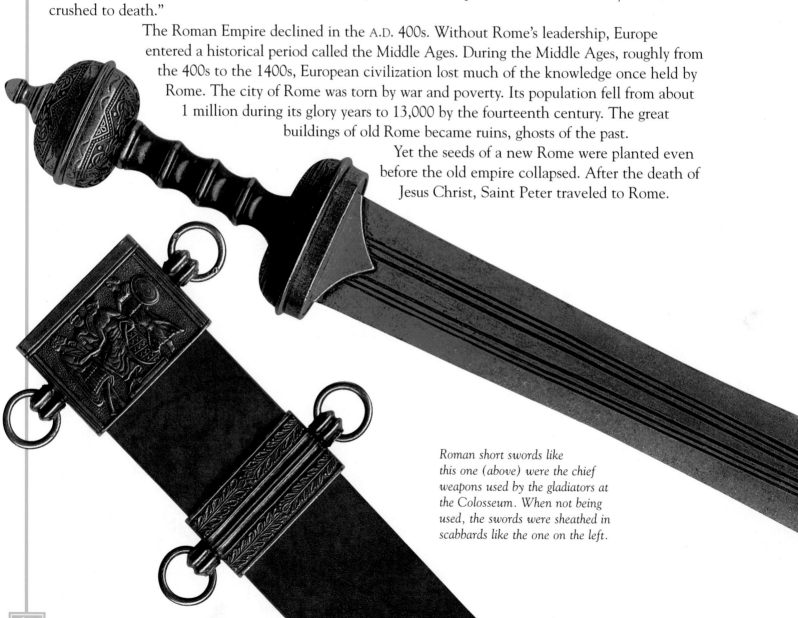

Roman short swords like this one (above) were the chief weapons used by the gladiators at the Colosseum. When not being used, the swords were sheathed in scabbards like the one on the left.

Left: *A relief of gladiators fighting wild beasts with their short swords*

Below: *Michelangelo da Caravaggio's painting the* Crucifixion of Saint Peter

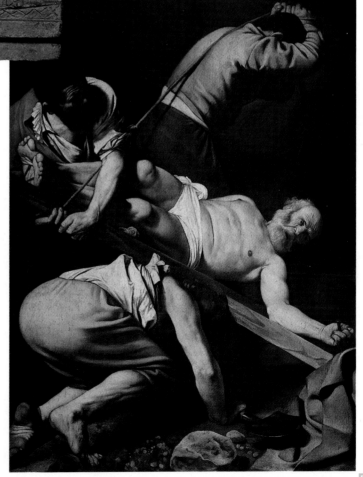

He was the simple fisherman who Christ declared would be the "rock" of His church. Peter, who preached Christianity, was executed by Roman authorities. At the time, Christians were considered to be enemies of the Roman state.

According to tradition, Saint Peter was buried on Vatican Hill in Rome. By the A.D. 300s, Christianity had become a major religion. A church was built over the spot believed to be Saint Peter's grave. Devout Christians traveled hundreds of miles to worship at St. Peter's Basilica. Rome thus became the center of the Roman Catholic faith.

THE REBIRTH

The French word *renaissance* means "rebirth." It describes a period from about A.D. 1400 to about 1600, when Europeans emerged from the Middle Ages to create a reborn world of art, architecture, science, and philosophy. Thought in the Middle Ages focused on God. The energy of the Renaissance concentrated on people and their creations. Italy led Europe in Renaissance achievement. During the Renaissance, Rome became what it is today—a huge, magnificent work of art.

Michelangelo (1475–1564) was the greatest of all the Renaissance artists. He was a true "Renaissance man," meaning that he was a genius in many areas. Michelangelo was a sculptor, a

Michelangelo designed the magnificent dome of St. Peter's Basilica, shown here from the inside (above) and the outside (left).

renaissance (RENN-UH-SAHNTS)
Michelangelo (MIGH-KULL-AN-JUH-LOH)
Sistine (SIS-TEEN)

painter, an architect, and a poet. In 1506, Catholic leader Pope Julius II chose Michelangelo to help draw plans for a new St. Peter's Basilica. Michelangelo designed the building's magnificent 450-foot (137-meter) dome. He also painted nine sweeping scenes from the Old Testament in the Sistine Chapel. One scene, "The Creation of Adam," shows God and Adam about to touch fingers. The touch will transfer the spark of life to the first human being. Michelangelo toiled for four years to paint the ceiling, "with my head turned back toward my spine," as he said. The Sistine Chapel, also on Vatican Hill, is one of Michelangelo's greatest achievements.

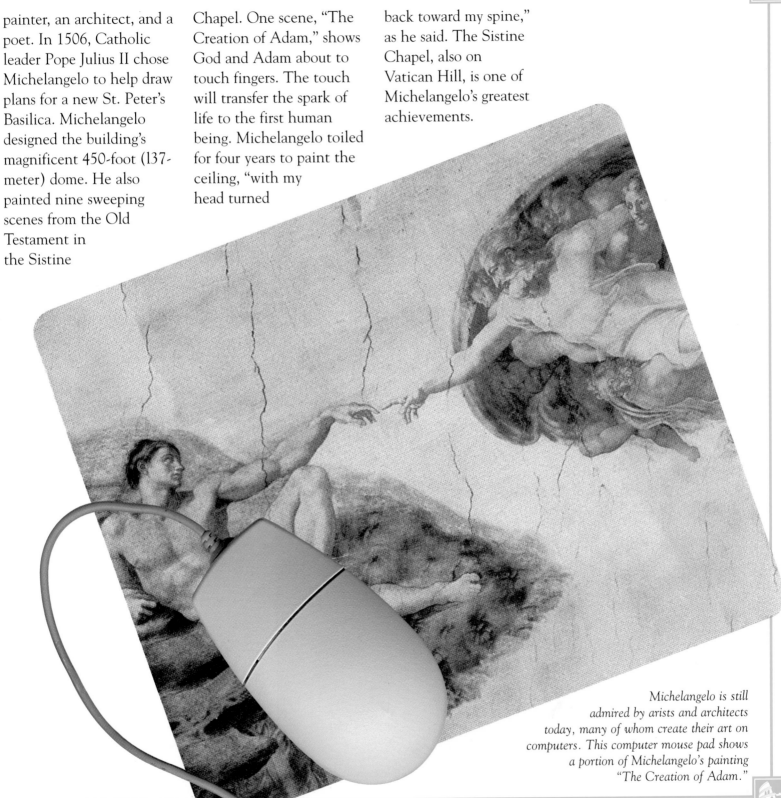

Michelangelo is still admired by arists and architects today, many of whom create their art on computers. This computer mouse pad shows a portion of Michelangelo's painting "The Creation of Adam."

Other Renaissance masters, including Raphael and Leonardo da Vinci, lived and worked in Rome. Gifted architects transformed the city by creating piazzas, churches, and fountains. Splendid palaces rose as homes for wealthy families. Many of the stones, statues, and marblework for the new structures were stripped from the ruins of ancient buildings. Thus, many buildings today have 2,000-year-old statues literally pressing through their walls.

Another art period, called the Baroque, was born in Rome in the 1600s. Baroque art is large in scale and rich with dramatic detail. Buildings of the period explode with designs on their outside walls. Great gushing fountains flowered in Rome in the Baroque years.

This painting by Renaissance artist Raphael, called Madonna di Foligno, *hangs in the Vatican.*

Raphael (RAH-FIGH-ELL)
Leonardo da Vinci
(LAY-OH-NAR-DOH DAH VEEN-CHEE)
Baroque (BUH-ROAK)
Borromini (BOAR-ROH-MEE-NEE)
Bernini (BAIR-NEE-NEE)

Rome's leading Baroque architects were Bernini and Borromini. Bernini's Fountain of the Four Rivers is a stunning example of the Baroque style. Today's Rome has more than 300 fountains, many of them masterpieces in stone and flowing water.

Above: Bernini's Triton Fountain in Piazza Barberini
Left: The statue at the center of the Fountain of Neptune in Piazza Navona is a copy of a statue designed by Bernini.

Swiss Guards

Vatican City has its own police force. They are the colorfully dressed Swiss Guards. It is believed that their yellow, orange, and blue uniforms were designed during the Renaissance by Michelangelo or Raphael.

MODERN ROME

For many centuries, there was no nation of Italy as we know it today. Instead, the Italian peninsula was a patchwork of small states. It was not until 1870 that Rome became the capital of a united Italy. The Catholic pope viewed the newly formed Italian government as a threat to church power. The pope shut himself up in church offices at Vatican Hill. Other popes followed the same policy. For sixty years, Catholic popes were known as "prisoners of the Vatican." Finally, in 1929, the church and the Italian government agreed to create a separate Vatican City within Rome. The Vatican—the world's smallest nation—was born.

Above: Vatican stamps and coins
Right: A priest in St. Peter's Square

Benito Mussolini

Heading the government during the Vatican negotiations was Benito Mussolini. He ruled Italy as a dictator. Mussolini left his mark on Rome by launching the construction of a suburb called E.U.R. The initials stood for a planned world exposition. The E.U.R. was carefully laid out with broad streets and grandiose office and apartment buildings. Today, the neighborhood is a vital part of Rome, even though it brings up the memory of a hated dictator. Angry Italians executed Mussolini in 1945.

After World War II, thousands of poor Italians from rural communities moved into Rome. High-rise buildings and suburbs were constructed to house the newcomers. Romans are passionate lovers of architecture. Many denounced the new buildings as faceless boxes. From around the world, visitors continued to pour into the capital. The vacationers gazed in awe at the artistic masterpieces the city had built over the ages. To the millions of tourists, Rome remains the Eternal City.

Benito Mussolini
(BAY-NEE-TOH MOO-SOH-LEE-NEE)
Via del Corso (VEE-AH DAIL COAR-SOH)

Via del Corso

Today, the Via del Corso is one of Rome's busiest streets. Its name means Way of the Race. During the Middle Ages, the street was a horse-racing track. The horses ran without riders. Romans stood on their balconies cheering the riderless animals forward.

An old saying goes, "When in Rome do as the Romans do." For ages, visitors have journeyed to the Eternal City. All have tried to live life as fully as do the people of Rome.

THE NON-ROMANS

The Spanish Steps lead up to a church built by the French. The neighborhood near the Spanish Steps houses many residents from Great Britain. An American-run school stands nearby. Sitting on the Spanish Steps are young backpackers from America and Europe. Along the steps, one hears English, French, German, Japanese, and a dozen other languages. The sound of the Italian language is a rarity. Rome is not merely the domain of the Romans. The Eternal City belongs to the world.

In the springtime, pots of colorful azaleas crowd the Spanish Steps, leaving little room for visitors in need of a rest.

During the summer tourist season, visitors to Rome outnumber natives. Even in the winter months, Rome is host to thousands of foreigners who live there year-round. Many of the transplanted Romans came originally as tourists. They fell in love with the city and decided to stay. A large number of the permanent foreign residents are writers and artists. The Italian capital has always inspired people to create. American writer Henry James moved to Rome in the 1870s. Delighted with the city, James wrote, "At last—for the first time—I live!"

Do the non-Roman residents ever become true Romans? Most foreigners would answer no. A true Roman has to be born in the Eternal City. As a child, he or she has to play hide-and-seek in a piazza designed by a Renaissance architect. Being Roman is a state of mind achieved only through the experience of living one's entire life in this unique city. This is not to say that Romans look down on foreign visitors. The reverse is true. Romans are immensely proud of their city. They enjoy showing it to guests. If a traveler asks street directions in a foreign language, a Roman will smile and try to help. Yet despite this friendliness, a foreigner remains a foreigner. Even other Italians complain that Rome is a closed society. Typical is the case of a businessman named Fanzone who was born in the northern Italian city of Milan. He says that after living in Rome for thirty years, he is still introduced as "Mr. Fanzone from Milan."

Do you speak English?
Parla inglese?

Where is the museum?
Dov' e il museo?

Milan (MIH-LONN)

An artist painting on a Rome sidewalk

GROWING UP ROMAN

Most Roman children, rich or poor, attend public schools. Catholic schools are available for families who wish to emphasize religious instruction. More than 90 percent of Romans are Catholics. But public schools are the norm.

Schools are divided into three stages. The first is *scuola elementare*, which is attended by children from first through fifth grades. Then the child graduates into *scuola media*, a middle school that serves sixth, seventh, and eighth grades. Beyond middle school, things get tough. Education beyond the eighth grade (age fourteen) is not mandatory in Italy. Still, most students want to go to the four-year high school program called the *liceo*. In order to be accepted at the liceo, one must pass a very demanding test. After surviving the exam, the student has to choose which category of high school to attend. One type of liceo specializes in history and literature while another emphasizes science and math.

Safety scissors like this pair are used by the youngest schoolchildren.

These children playing a game go to a scuola elementare.

scuola elementare
(SKWAW-LAH AY-LAY-MAIN-TAH-RAY)
scuola media
(SKWAW-LAH MEH-DEE-AH)
liceo (LEE-CHAY-OH)

Of course, Rome offers children a world of lively activities after school. In the heart of the city is the Villa Borghese, one of Europe's finest parks. Children begin going to the park when they are toddlers. The Puppet Theater of Villa Borghese gives performances nearly every day. Older children go to Luna Park in the E.U.R. district. Luna Park is an amusement center famous for its gigantic Ferris wheel. All young people enjoy eating at the tiny ice-cream parlors that dot the neighborhood. Rome is said to have the finest ice cream in the world.

On warm days during the spring and summer, Romans enjoy relaxing in the beautiful gardens at the Villa Borghese.

> *Villa Borghese*
> (VEE-LAH BOAR-GAY-ZAY)
> *Luna* (LOO-NAH)

Teenage girls like to go shopping in groups. There are no American-style shopping malls in central Rome. Instead, the girls board the bus and go to shopping districts such as the Villa Gregoriana. There, the streets are lined with clothing stores selling the latest fashions. Shoppers must beware, however. Prices at the trendy clothing stores are steep. So the teenagers go to to the city's many flea markets to look for bargain clothing.

Getting around the hectic streets is a challenge for children of any age. Most children walk to school. If the school is far away, they take a public bus or ride the subway. There are no school buses in Rome. After school, children hop on their bicycles and race off to the nearest park.

Crowds flock to the Sunday morning Porta Portese market, one of the largest flea markets in Europe.

University students gather after classes in what is known as the student quarter.

The Jewish Ghetto

At one time, all of Rome's Jews were forced to live in a very small neighborhood made up of narrow, twisting streets. There, they made meager livings working as tailors and peddlers. Today, that old Jewish Quarter is a wonderful neighborhood for leisurely walking. The narrow streets discourage car traffic.

Cycling is a passion in all of Italy. Over the years, Italian bicyclists have won dozens of medals in the Olympic Games. Less popular are skateboards and in-line skates. Many Roman streets are made of cobblestones. Cobblestones make for a bumpy, dangerous ride on skates. Older children dream about some day owning their own *motorino* (moped or motorbike). Mopeds are expensive, but middle-class families buy them for teenagers. The youngster is advised to put two or three locks on the motorino. The bikes are prime targets for thieves.

One of Rome's many bicyclists stops for a drink at an old fountain.

Villa Gregoriana
(VEEL-lah GRAY-GOAR-EE-ON-AH)
motorino (MOH-TOH-REE-NOH)

PLEASURES OF
THE ROMAN WAY

Hungry? Better not try to wolf down your food in a Roman restaurant. To a Roman, preparing and serving food is an art form. Great art cannot be rushed to completion. Yes, there are fast-food establishments in Rome. Young people seem to like hamburger and fried-chicken places. But Romans generally find the meal-a-minute concept to be distasteful. In the early 1990s, a McDonald's opened in a dignified, old restaurant district. The opening almost caused a riot.

trattoria
(TROT-TOH-REE-AH)
ristorante
(REE-STOH-RONN-TAY)
crostata di frutta
(CROH-STAH-TAH DEE FROOT-TAH)

An open-air restaurant on the Piazza Navona

These Romans are enjoying a leisurely meal at an outdoor restaurant.

Restaurants are listed in two categories: *trattorias* or *ristorantes*. In theory, trattorias are smaller and offer fewer choices on their menus. Tourists, however—and most Romans—can't tell the difference between the two places. A typical dinner comes in three courses: pasta, meat or fish, and dessert. The pasta course alone is a meal in itself. When Romans dine in groups of eight to ten, waiters bring out huge bowls of spaghetti covered with sauce. The bowls are passed around the table. Diners scoop out the pasta with forks and put it on their plates. Expect the courses to arrive at your table at a leisurely pace. Romans go to restaurants to chat as well as to eat. No one demands quick service. But the food is wonderful. For dessert, try a *crostata di frutta*, a tart filled with delicious fruit.

Romans are sports lovers. Soccer is easily the city's favorite spectator sport. Two soccer teams compete for the fans' loyalties. A team called Roma is favored by the people of central Rome. Another team, Lazio, finds its supporters in the suburbs. Twice a year, the two teams play each other. Game days are like a civil war. The soccer rivalry also touches on a clash between rich and poor. In the United States, people with the most money tend to live in the suburbs. In Rome, the situation is reversed. Wealthy Romans live in the inner city, and the poor inhabit the suburbs. Still, soccer competition is usually friendly. Supporters of Roma enjoy teasing the suburban Lazio fans by equating them with farmers. When a Lazio rooter goes to a game, a Roma fan might shout out, "Hey, where did you park your tractor?"

Since early in the twentieth century, Rome has been the "Hollywood" of the Italian movie industry. Shortly after World War II, several movies made in Rome became classics beloved by international audiences. One such movie was *The Bicycle Thief* (1948). It told the

Soccer, the most popular sport in Rome, is also the most popular sport in the world.

Roma (ROH-MAH)
Lazio (LOT-SEE-OH)

bittersweet story of a Roman factory worker and his young son desperately trying to find a stolen bicycle. In the 1960s, a huge studio complex stood in suburban Rome. The complex churned out movies with American western themes. Critics dubbed these films "spaghetti westerns." Today, filmmaking continues to be a very special artistic expression in the capital. The movie industry adds luster to the city's reputation.

The Sweet Life

Italian film director Federico Fellini has been called a "poet with a camera." His films often poked fun at Rome's powerful upper classes. Fellini's most famous movie was produced in 1961. One scene showed a glamorous woman splashing about in Rome's Trevi Fountain in the middle of the night. The film was called *La Dolce Vita* ("The Sweet Life").

La Dolce Vita
(LAH DOAL-chay VEE-tah)

Roman children—boys and girls alike—are active in sports from a very young age.

41

Tourism is Rome's largest industry. Tourists come to see the ancient sites and the works of the Renaissance. Serious Roman Catholics make pilgrimages to the Vatican. Other vacationers enjoy shopping and dining in world-class restaurants. It could be said that Rome's population consists of two classes—Romans and visitors. Romans treat guests with warmth. Visitors enjoy a vacation they will never forget.

MEMORIES OF THE ANCIENTS

History surrounds visitors to the Forum in central Rome. It was here that powerful leaders such as Julius Caesar conferred with senators. Their decisions sealed the fate of the known world. Today, the Forum is a collection of time-worn columns and other ruins. Tourists as well as native Romans enjoy walking through these remnants. Visitors stretch their imaginations and recall an era when there was no power on earth other than Rome.

Leaders in ancient times built grand houses on Palatine Hill. Indeed, the word *Palatine* gave rise to the English word *palace*. Today, the crumbling ruins of those once marvelous houses each have stories to tell. Modern visitors enter a tunnel built by the half-mad emperor Nero.

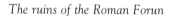
The ruins of the Roman Forun

A statue of Julius Caesar

Perhaps Nero planned to use the tunnel as an escape route from his sumptuous palace. Nero committed suicide in A.D. 68, while Romans rioted against his rule. Also on the hill are the remains of a house built by the emperor Domitian. That house had mirrors on the wall so that Domitian could see the approach of an enemy. In A.D. 96, Domitian was murdered by a group of men who were smuggled into the house at night with the help of his wife. A prominent ruin on Palatine Hill is a stadium called the Circus Maximus. In its heyday, the Circus Maximus hosted a wildly popular series of chariot races. The races lasted fifteen days or more.

The Palace of Domitian on Palatine Hill

The Temple of the Vestal Virgins

One of the more impressive ruins at the Forum is the Temple of the Vestal Virgins. In ancient times, the eternal fire of Rome burned there night and day. The fire was tended by women who vowed to have no contact with men. If they broke their vow, the man involved was strangled and the woman was buried alive.

Palatine (PAL-UH-TIGHN)
Nero (NEER-OH)
Domitian (DOH-MEE-SHUNN)
Circus Maximus (SIR-KUSS MAX-IH-MUSS)

The Colosseum is the most outstanding reminder of Rome's golden age. Here, too, visitors use their imaginations to envision the empire's glory as well as its darker side. Picture the Colosseum packed with mobs of cheering people. A trumpet blast silences the crowd. Gladiators march in, armed with swords and spears. The gladiators face the emperor's box. In unison they chant, "Hail Caesar! We who are about to die salute you." Then, with a roar from the crowd, the "games" begin. The last of these gladiatorial contests was held in the A.D. 400s. During the Renaissance, builders took stone and marble from the Colosseum's walls to construct palaces. Then, in the 1700s, Pope Benedict XIV ordered the builders to stop stripping the ancient structure. Christians had been slaughtered in the arena. The pope wanted the Colosseum to be preserved as a monument to Christian martyrs. The Colosseum has remained a monument ever since.

A view of the interior of the Colosseum

*Left: The Colosseum
illuminated at night
Above: A detail of the
Colosseum at dusk*

THE VATICAN

The Vatican, often called Vatican City, is only 108 acres (44 hectares) in area. Many shopping malls in American suburbs are larger. The permanent population of Vatican City is less than 1,000. Yet this tiny state has its own post office, its own army, and its own railroad station. It is the residence of the pope and the spiritual center for 1 billion Roman Catholics around the world. Vatican City is also a celebration of paintings, architecture, sculpture, and history. No visit to Rome is complete without a Vatican tour.

Opposite page: St. Peter's Square
Left: A night view of the Vatican
and the River Tiber
Right: A Roman Catholic rosary,
a string of beads used in counting prayers
Below: A Swiss Guard in the Vatican

St. Peter's Square

St. Peter's Basilica is the world's largest Christian church. It took nearly 150 years to build the church. No other building on earth contains the combined work of so many masterful architects, artists, and sculptors. Its most spectacular feature is the Great Dome, designed by Michelangelo. On clear days, the 450-foot (137-meter) dome can be seen from any part of Rome. By law, no building in the city may be higher. Inside St. Peter's is Michelangelo's famous sculpture *The Pietà.* The statue shows Mary cradling the body of Jesus. The magnificent bronze canopy above the altar is a creation of the Baroque master Bernini. The canopy features twisted columns that invite the eye and inspire the soul. Outside is St. Peter's Square, also designed by Bernini.

A miniature replica of Michelangelo's sculpture, The Pietà

*Michelangelo's famous
Sistine Chapel paintings*

The square is flanked by columns that stand in a semicircular formation. The columns represent the embracing arms of the mother church.

The Vatican museums hold one of the world's greatest collections of paintings and sculpture.

Guided tours of the museums take up to five hours, but can cover just a fraction of the artwork. Chapels within are graced with paintings by artists including Raphael, Titian, and Leonardo da Vinci. Most guided tours end at the Sistine Chapel. On the chapel's walls and ceilings spread Michelangelo's famous series of paintings. They present nine events from the Old Testament. Visitors to the Sistine Chapel leave breathless with wonder.

Pietà (PYAY-TAH)
Titian (TEE-shen)

TREASURES OF THE ETERNAL CITY

Getting lost in Rome is fun. Around every corner is a surprise—a grand church, a 500-year-old palace, a museum, or a bubbling fountain. People who are momentarily lost open their eyes wider to capture surprises. Above all, Rome is a city to be looked at.

Certainly, a church designed to catch the eye is the Santa Maria in Trastevere. Dating to the A.D. 400s, the Santa Maria in Trastevere has been rebuilt and added to many times. For that reason, it incorporates several artistic periods and commands the attention of art historians. The Church of St. Peter in Chains holds two revered objects. The first is the statue *Moses*, by Michelangelo. The second is a length of ancient chain that is kept in a bronze and crystal case near the altar. According to legend, it was once two chains. One chain bound Saint Peter when he was a prisoner in Jerusalem. A second chain held him just before his crucifixion in Rome. When the two chains were put together, they magically fused into one length.

Trastevere (TRAH-STAY-vay-ray)
Cosmedin (COAZ-MAID-on)
Venezia (VAY-NAIT-see-ah)
Madonna (MAH-DOAN-ah)

Michelangelo's sculpture Moses is in the Church of St. Peter in Chains.

The Metro

Getting around Rome is easy on the subway (the Metro). It is clean, safe, and fast. But Rome's Metro consists of only two lines. Efforts to dig more lines are hampered by the fact that the remains of ancient civilizations lie below the modern streets. These treasured relics cannot simply be bulldozed out of the ground. Instead, they must be carefully excavated by archaeologists. For this reason, extending the Metro is a difficult undertaking.

The Church of Santa Maria in Cosmedin is also connected with a legend. Attached to the outside wall of the church is a large stone mask with a hole in the center. The hole is called the "Mouth of Truth." It is said that if a person holds a hand in the mouth and tells a lie, the mouth will chop down on the liar's fingers. Test the legend only if you dare!

Rome's splendid palaces were built for powerful merchants and popes. The massive Venezia Palace was constructed in the mid-1400s. The building's Renaissance influence can be seen in its elegantly arched windows. In the 1930s, dictator Benito Mussolini used Venezia Palace as his office. The palace now houses an art museum. The Borghese Palace is another marvelous Renaissance structure. Only a portion of the building is open to the public because, to this day,

The stone mask called the "Mouth of Truth" at the Church of Santa Maria in Cosmedin

Medici (MEH-DEE-CHEE)
Doria (DOAR-EE-UH)

it remains the property of the Borghese family. The Madonna Palace was once owned by the powerful Medici family. The Medicis were merchants and art

collectors. Today, the Madonna Palace is headquarters for the Italian Senate. Palace life in all its splendor comes alive at the Doria Palace. The palace

grounds contain 1,000 rooms, 5 courtyards, and 4 ornate staircases. Also in the Doria Palace is a Baroque chapel and a spectacular ballroom.

A colossal statue of Constantine once stood in the Basilica of Constantine and Maxentius. Parts of this huge statue (left) can now be seen in the courtyard of the Palazzo dei Conservatori.

Marcus Aurelius (MAR-kuss aw-RAY-lee-uss)
Villa Gulia (VEEL-lah JOO-lee-ah)
Etruscan (EH-TRUSS-ken)

This statue of Marcus Aurelius (right), once the focal point of Capitoline Square, has been restored and now stands in the Capitoline Museum.

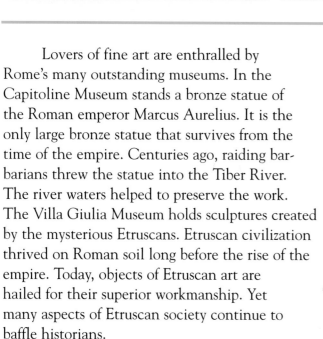

Lovers of fine art are enthralled by Rome's many outstanding museums. In the Capitoline Museum stands a bronze statue of the Roman emperor Marcus Aurelius. It is the only large bronze statue that survives from the time of the empire. Centuries ago, raiding barbarians threw the statue into the Tiber River. The river waters helped to preserve the work. The Villa Giulia Museum holds sculptures created by the mysterious Etruscans. Etruscan civilization thrived on Roman soil long before the rise of the empire. Today, objects of Etruscan art are hailed for their superior workmanship. Yet many aspects of Etruscan society continue to baffle historians.

Tourists sitting at Trevi Fountain

Poems, paintings, and even symphonies have praised Rome's fountains. The fountains were originally built to fill household jugs. Today, the creations stand as a glorious form of public art. The Fountain of Neptune entertains people in the historic Piazza Navona. The Triton Fountain is the centerpiece for the Piazza Barberini.

Certainly the most popular of all Rome's fountains is the Trevi. It is a fantasy of gods, goddesses, horses, and heroes all bathed in flowing water. There is said to be magic in the Trevi. To benefit from the magic, people must stand with their backs toward the fountain. Then they throw a coin over their shoulders and into the waters. If this ritual is performed correctly, they will return to Rome. Tourists from every part of the globe carry out this coin-throwing custom on the last night of their stay. All wish that some day they will come back to the Eternal City.

A detail of the Fountain of Neptune

FAMOUS LANDMARKS

The Trevi Fountain at dusk

The Pantheon

The Arch of Constantine

The Pantheon

The best preserved of ancient Rome's monuments, the Pantheon was completed in A.D. 125. It was intended as a temple honoring all the Roman gods. White marble statues of Jupiter and the goddess Minerva once stood here. Over the centuries, the building has been used as a military fortress, a Christian church, and as a fish and vegetable market. The great Renaissance artist Raphael is buried beneath the Pantheon. Raphael's many admirers still bring him flowers.

Piazza Navona

This popular gathering place is a beautiful Baroque square that has been largely unchanged for hundreds of years. Today, it is a restful city island, one of the places where car traffic is forbidden. Some 2,000 years ago, it was a racetrack for chariots and horses. Its curved ends reflect the one-time racecourse design.

Trevi Fountain

The most famous fountain in Rome, the Trevi is a wonder of marble, stone, and flowing water. Make a wish, throw a coin in the fountain, and you will some day return to the Eternal City.

The Spanish Steps

The graceful cascade of steps, built in 1723, is among Rome's top tourist attractions. Nearly all visitors bring back pictures of themselves standing in front of the Spanish Steps. Climb the steps, all 136 of them, and you arrive at the Trinità dei Monti, an elegant church. The streets around the Spanish Steps are lined with the city's most expensive shops.

The Colosseum

The proud symbol of ancient Rome is shaped much like a modern football stadium. In fact, modern football stadiums are built in imitation of this structure. The Colosseum once hosted bloody spectacles such as animal slaughter and gladiator combat. But even at the height of the old empire, many Roman intellectuals denounced pageants at the Colosseum. The intellectuals claimed the Colosseum shows were the government's way of keeping citizens peaceful by giving them "bread and circuses."

The interior of the Colosseum

Above: The Spanish Steps
Right: Castel Sant' Angelo as seen
from the Ponte Sant' Angelo

Arch of Constantine

This graceful arch honors the Roman emperor Constantine. Late in his life, Emperor Constantine converted to Christianity. Thereafter, Constantine allowed the religion to expand in Roman territory. Nearby are other reminders of the empire, including the Arch of Titus and the many ruins of the Roman Forum.

Ponte Sant' Angelo

The St. Angelo Bridge spans the Tiber River and is Rome's oldest and most beautiful bridge. The statues of Saint Peter, Saint Paul, and ten angels stand along its parapets. The bridge reminds people of the importance of the Tiber River, which winds through the heart of the city.

Castel Sant' Angelo

Directly across the St. Angelo Bridge stands this imposing castle. In ancient times, it was a mausoleum. Then, in A.D. 590, Pope Gregory the Great claimed that he saw an angel above the site. The pope ordered a chapel to be built. The chapel evolved into the familiar round building that now serves as a museum.

Vatican City

The world's tiniest independent nation, the Vatican is the headquarters for the Roman Catholic faith. Devout Catholics come here on religious pilgrimages. The pilgrims experience the thrill of worshiping at St. Peter's and perhaps seeing the pope. The Vatican and its museums hold unmatched artistic treasures.

Santa Maria in Trastevere

This is the first church in Rome to be dedicated to the Virgin Mary. On its inside walls are marvelous ceramic mosaics.

San Pietro in Montorio

It is believed that this church was built on the spot where Saint Peter was crucified. A tiny temple in the courtyard has a hole where people can peek through and see the ground where Saint Peter's cross once stood.

FAST FACTS

POPULATION

City:	2,830,569
Metropolitan Area:	3,400,000

AREA   58 square miles (150 square kilometers)

LAND   Most of ancient Rome was built on seven hills; the modern city embraces more than twenty hills. Buildings are crowded close together, but there are no true skyscrapers. By law, no building may exceed 450 feet (137 meters), the height of St. Peter's dome. The Tiber River winds through the heart of the city. Rome has many parks. Some parks were once private gardens owned by wealthy families. The Villa Borghese, opened in 1902, is the city's most popular park.

CLIMATE   Rome enjoys a gentle climate that encourages outdoor activity such as sidewalk cafes and open-air street markets. The average July temperature is 78 degrees Fahrenheit (25 degrees Celsius); the average January temperature is 45 degrees Fahrenheit (7 degrees Celsius). Rain is most common in the fall and winter months. Midsummer days can be uncomfortably hot, but the evenings are often cooled by a refreshing sea breeze.

INDUSTRIES   Rome is not a factory center. Most workers hold tourist-related jobs or are employed by the government. The city has an estimated 600,000 office workers. Industries employ only about one-fifth of the workforce. The city's industrial plants are concentrated in the outskirts, mostly in the northwest. The factories produce processed foods, textiles, and clothing.

CHRONOLOGY

753 B.C.
According to legend, Rome is founded by twin brothers, Romulus and Remus.

509 B.C.
Romans drive the Etruscans out of their settlement and establish a republic.

264–146 B.C.
In a series of three wars, Rome defeats its chief rival, Carthage, and becomes the greatest power in the Mediterranean region.

27 B.C.
Rome becomes an empire; Augustus is the first emperor.

A.D. 96–180
The Roman Empire reaches its height.

395
The Roman Empire splits into two parts—east and west; the decline of Rome begins.

476
The last Roman emperor dies mysteriously, possibly at the hands of his own warriors.

852
Walls are built surrounding the Vatican; the popes' power over Rome increases.

About 1400
The Renaissance, a thrilling period in art and learning, begins in Italy and sweeps through Europe.

Feeding the city's pigeons is a popular activity for Romans young and old.

1506
The first stone of the new St. Peter's Basilica is laid by Pope Julius II.

1541
Michelangelo completes his work on the Sistine Chapel.

Late 1500s
A new style of art known as Baroque originates in Rome.

1870
Rome becomes the capital of a united Italy.

1929
The Vatican is made an independent state.

1944
Allied armies free Rome from occupation by German forces during World War II.

1960
Rome hosts the Olympic Games.

1990
The World Cup Soccer Championships are held in Rome.

1994
Pope John Paul II announces that the year 2000 will be a Holy Year, meaning that millions of Catholic pilgrims will come to worship at St. Peter's; Rome begins massive projects designed to ease traffic congestion and clean up ancient monuments in preparation for the Holy Year.

ROME

	A	B	C	D	E	F	G	H	I	J	K
1						Villa Giulia Museum					
2						Piazza del Popolo	Villa Borghese				
3										Porta Pia	
4	Vatican City VATICAN HILL	St. Peter's Basilica	Castel Sant' Angelo		Borghese Palace		Piazza di Spagna / Spanish Steps	Triton Fountain / Piazza Barberini			
5	Piazza San Pietro	Ponte Sant' Angelo		Piazza Navona	Madonna Palace / Pantheon	Trevi Fountain	Vittorio Emanuele Monument				
6					Venezia Palace	Capitoline Museum	Trajan's Column / Temple of the Vestal Virgins	Church of St. Peter in Chains			
7				Santa Maria in Trastevere	Isola Tiberina	Santa Maria in Cosmedin	Forum / PALATINE HILL	Arch of Constantine / Colosseum			
8				San Pietro in Montorio		Circus Maximus					

Tiber River

Via del Corso

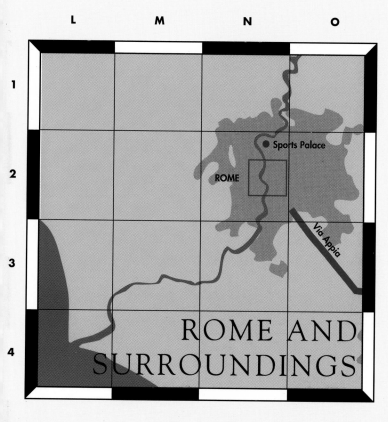

GLOSSARY

archaeologist: A person who studies objects from past civilizations

barbarian: An uncivilized person

domain: Home, realm

feline: Cat

legitimate theater: Theater where live plays are performed

mandatory: Required by law

Middle Ages: Period in European history dating from the late 400s to the mid-1400s

ornate: Lavishly designed, ornamental

pilgrimage: Journey to a sacred place

rural: Pertaining to the country or farming regions

siesta: Afternoon nap

sumptuous: Large and splendid

zenith: Highest point

Picture Identifications

Cover: The Colosseum; statue on Ponte Sant' Angelo, St. Peter's in background; Roman boys
Title Page: Young visitors at the Capitoline Museum
Pages 4-5: St. Peter's Basilica as seen from the Tiber River
Pages 8-9: An open-air market
Page 9: Opera glasses
Pages 18-19: The Roman Forum viewed from Capitoline Hill, the Colosseum in the background
Page 19: Statue of Romulus and Remus with wolf
Pages 30-31: Man reading a newspaper at a Piazza Navona fountain
Pages 42-43: Vatican City and St. Peter's Basilica at sunrise

NDEX

age numbers in boldface type indicate illustrations

TO FIND OUT MORE

BOOKS

Bonomi, Kathryn. *Italy*. New York: Chelsea House, 1991.

Corbishley, Mike. *The Roman World*. New York and London: Warwick Press, 1986.

Hewitt, Sally. *The Romans: Activities, Crafts, History*. Chicago: Children's Press, 1995.

James, Simon. *Ancient Rome*. Eyewitness Book series. New York: Alfred A. Knopf, 1990.

Lace, William W. *Michelangelo*. San Diego: Lucent Books, 1993.

Muhlberger, Richard. *What Makes a Raphael a Raphael*. New York: Viking, 1993.

Mulvihill, Margaret. *Mussolini and Italian Fascism*. New York: Franklin Watts, 1990.

Powell, Anton. *Renaissance Italy*. New York and London: Warwick Press, 1980.

Ridgwell, Jenny. *A Taste of Italy*. New York: Thomson Learning, 1993.

Steele, Philip. *Food and Feasts in Ancient Rome*. New York: New Discovery Books, 1994.

Stein, R. Conrad. *Italy*. Enchantment of the World series. Chicago: Childrens Press, 1984.

Wood, Tim. *The Renaissance*. New York: Viking, 1993.

ONLINE SITES

La Ragnatela
http://www.ytko.co.uk/ragnatela/
An art gallery, with beautiful photos of places and things in Italy. Plus, many great links to things Italian.

Leonardo da Vinci Museum
http://cellini.leonardo.net/museum/main.html#start
From the Main Gallery, move to any of the four "wings" to see the *Mona Lisa, The Last Supper,* Leonardo's designs for weapons and flying machines, and a historical exhibit.

Roman Imperial Architecture
http://www.wisc.edu/arth/ah201/18.imperialarchitecture.2.html
More great photos and a bit of history: the Colosseum, the Forum, the Temple of Mars, Pompeii, and many links.

Roma 2000
http://www.roma2000.it/english.html
A really fun site, this virtual tour of Rome will take you to museums, monuments, restaurants, hotels, and more—all with a clickable map. And the angels flap their wings!

Rome
http://www.mi.cnr.it/WOI/deagosti/regions/lazio2.html#Rome
Learn about all aspects of Rome, its rich history, culture, and attractions.

Vatican City
http://www.christusrex.org/www1/icons/vatican.html
Visit the country within a city—maps, flags, museums, history, facts and figures, speeches by the pope, and photos.

Virtual Rome
http://www.pacificnet.net/virtualrome/village.html
Visit virtual museums, learn about the history of the Roman Empire, create your own Web page, take a tour of the solar system, and play alien war games!

The Webfoot's Guide to Italy
http://www.webfoot.com/travel/guides/italy/italy.html
Links to a factbook, satellite weather images, Italian money, maps, the current time, the flag, and many other sites.

Windows on Italy
http://www.mi.cnr.it/WOI
A ton of great information about the country, its history, government, and people. Links to each of the regions and towns.

ABOUT THE AUTHOR

R. Conrad Stein was born and grew up in Chicago. After serving in the Marine Corps, he attended the University of Illinois, where he received a degree in history. He has published more than eighty books for young readers. Mr. Stein lives in Chicago with his wife and their daughter Janna.